Sweet No
Stuff

Anya Vitaliev

BookLeaf
Publishing

Presentation by *BookLeaf Publishing*

Web: www.bookleafpub.com

E-mail: info@bookleafpub.com

ISBN: 9789357696500

First edition 2022

DEDICATION

Thank you to Julia, you crossed my path and brought a new kind of inspiration to me. You helped me see myself as my own artistic muse.

Thank you Steady & Head-Man, my co-habitants in the Garden of Eden (if you know you know.)

And literally everyone else- thanks for making life a little bit interesting. Hope you know who you are.

From my heart,
Bless you

PREFACE

I've just moved to Brixton where I can feel that feeling I get when I'm on my pathway, in the right direction. I would compare the feeling to when you're a child and you'd wake up on you're birthday, knowing that day was all about you. Or when your crush finally reveals (not just in your imagination) that they also have a crush on you. It's like that except you cant put your finger on exactly what's so exciting. You just feel kind of... special. This feeling has been my guiding light, very little distraction from rational thinking trends to occur with me anyway.

So when I got here, on my fourth flat move of the year (because of a series of unfortunate flat mates, to be frank)- I finally felt like it was all about leading me to that spot. The shit that I learned on the way to that morning I woke up for the first time in Brixton, was all necessary to form me into what I felt like then - perfection, in the right place at the right time. A rare feeling and somewhat a peculiar sense of euphoria, which was followed by these strange intuitions/prophecies my mind created, for lack of a better term... started coming true. The only reason I'm writing this book and you're reading it is because I think.. I wished it. My first morning in Brixton I walked all the way to work, and I felt connected. My street is right in the Center, and the room is a shoe box to be able to live in such a sick spot- but due to that, the crack heads (of which Brixton has plenty) also think my street is one of the best ones to live. And luckily, to me I already know they're completely harmless, just people who got lost. I've never really been too afraid of talking to strangers, even when in some situations I've realised I definitely shouldn't have in hindsight. However the beautiful occurrences where you thank your lucky stars you denied every socially engrained fear in you because of the urge to speak to someone that you just randomly, effortlessly get sometimes is something I've come to believe in very strongly. I've met some of my best friends and had some of the most exciting encounters that way- because I can't deny my gut feeling in these situations. People are just everything to me. All that "we are one" crap- I haven't figured out how, but I reckon it's true. I ran into four old lovers that week, I got what I am happy to call closure of sorts (from at least three of them … still maybe a bit sad about one of them… for now) and it allowed me to begin a new chapter- I could mark it with this feeling and my observations of how bloody strange and coincidental everything felt that week. You know what I'm talking about? I just felt kind of special.

One of the Brixton 'crack-heads' caught me as I was walking down my road today. He was, I kid you not- in robes. He obviously spooked me a bit when he called out for me but I took off my headphones to at least acknowledge him. My mum raised me this way. I said hello and went to leave- but he told me not to not be afraid. He kept repeating to 'please not be afraid.' And I was, still shaking but decided to just trust him. He took my hand and held it. I held my breathe, regretting my decision immediately. Yesss this "should" be the part where you run away from the messiah looking mofo but I just don't have enough priorities to think that he can fully ruin my day, I wasn't doing anything. If he has nothing, and asks me not to be afraid - for a few minutes, that's the least I could give him. He smelled of piss but when I looked into his eyes, he was completely sane. At least, in his own way- his eyes were trustworthy. If it weren't for the circumstances, and the smell, he'd probably have quite an easy time getting people to listen to him. And because I trusted him enough- (I'm asking you to trust my judgement... enough on this one) I listened to what he wanted, seemingly desperately, wanted to say to me. He told me "you are special. You must know you are special. "My heart leaped for a second, this was a tickling thing to hear- even from a crack head i've never seen before. I tried to be my open self, be human with him-but like, sum it up, shove it in a nutshell for him. I told him "yeah.. sometimes I think I'm special but then I'm not sure" and he told me "please, you must trust this feeling." He complimented my eyes and my smile (but like in a way that wasn't actually even slightly creepy (take it from the girl who's hand he was holding.) I thanked him, and he thanked me for not being afraid- although he said he could sense a little fear, which was very real. He said that, and I trusted him even more, I wanted to follow this moment through. I told him that I'm writing a book of poetry and these are the kinds of things I want to be even more open to because life keeps throwing mysteries at me and there's something going on for sure, so I make an effort to pay attention. I thanked him for approaching peacefully.

He said he needed to tell me something and went to his pile of possessions to bring a book out, a huge, heavy looking book. My first thought was obviously to roll my eyes- I told him not to start on the bible stuff incase I end up getting triggered. He didn't know what I meant by trigerred but told me "it's not religion" so doubtfully I just told him to continue and I'd stay calm. He opened his book to a very specific page, which didn't take him long to find at all. He took one of my hands again and told me- "you are special. The best way to write your poetry is to live it.." And then pointed to a passage, half way down one of the rice paper pages. In a fashion that I want to clarify, was not similar to the guys' with megaphones outside of tube stations- I read it aloud right next to him on the busy Brixton street:

"A gracious woman retaineth honour: and strong men retain riches.

The Merciful man doeth good to his own soul: but he that is cruel troubleth his own flesh.

As a jewel of gold in a swine's snout, so is a fair woman which is without discretion.

There is that scattereth and yet increaseth; and there is that with-holdeth more than is meet, but it tendeth to poverty.

The liberal soul shall be fat: and he that watereth shall be watered also himself.

He that withholdeth corn, the people shall curse him: but blessing shall be upon the head of him that selleth it.

He that diligently seeketh good procureth favour: but he that seeketh mischief, it shall come unto him.

He that trusteth in his riches shall fall but the righteous shall flourish as a branch."

My interpretation of the passage, and the fact he flagged me down to read it to him- spoke to me. It did the same thing art does, where it soaks into your soul with grace that you can't ever see, but that strongly makes itself known in feeling. You couldn't before have put your finger on that feeling, didn't think others' knew existed. I went out to go give him money later but he had gone. Not even spent the night on our streets' finest porch. I hope he's okay, as much as a crack head really can be. I think he hopes the same for me, in his own little version of reality. And I'll choose to believe him, and count that meeting as a sign that I am special, at-least in my own little reality. I shit you not- these funny things, I think are the universe or something... keep happening to me. This one came to me, not only to inspire me- but seemingly to encourage me and remind me of certain things. This book/art-piece is coincidentally me trying to no longer 'with holdeth my corn,' if you will.

Whose to tell me these things aren't signs? The clues I'm
looking for? The meaning of life?
Hints to the answer
I live to uncover
But might never find?
Then, this could just be some kind of
Coping mechanism…
But I don't really mind.

Ur an enigma

Too hot to handle;

The fire in her eyes-

But she saw the world

In a way she kept

Struggling to describe

Too pitchy to sing about,

No angels' voice

could compare

To the way things would sound in her head

Here, there and like literally everywhere

Too emotional to act out;

The way she felt sometimes,

To capture the ineffable essence

Of why she just kinda trusted life

Too delicate a beauty

For great painters to paint,

To reflect the light she saw things in

(what was keeping her awake)

Too hard to write about;

What she thought she knew.

Too small a vocabulary

Exists

To give anyone a clue

Her masterpiece was somewhere

But she wanted

a map towards the way

She could make it into matter

And, painting wasn't really

Her thing anyway

Ur my Crush

The World is my oyster

How I fucking dread the taste.

The only town I ever painted

thought it was a disgrace.

I could puff 'the magic dragon'

but we'll never fly away

because the sun is always shining

and I am severely burned

by it's rays.

"Make it into lemonade," they say

but they really need to stop.

Life's little box of chocolates

put me into anaphylactic shock.

You're supposed to go up

from rock bottom

but I am going steady.

And if beauty be

in the eye of the beholder,

then why won't you just

behold me, already?

Ur my everything

Reclaiming things

(We'll call it)

Is my new hobby.

I've decided I'd like to

Retrace the steps

We walked all over together-

Delicate craftsmanship but

They were looking worn and shoddy.

It's gunna be like up-cycling but less about aesthetic.

I've been avoiding the places we went together and
it's beginning to feel a bit pathetic.

You can't have

all the best songs that never fail to make weep-

I'm going to hear them and think of others-

I'm going to hear them and think of me.

Of course, I'll never completely

 transform the antiques,

nostalgia is nice- You don't get it from all these new fangled things.

You can refurbish an old house

But if it's haunted, the walls will never forget what it used to be. You were once a beautiful flower to me. How when you left the sun light, was it me who couldn't breathe?

I sat afterwards, for a long time in the dark,

It turns out that things were blossoming

From the seeds you planted in me

over the time apart.

At first I couldn't I hear one chord of that song or take the short-cut down your street.

Now I want my freedom back,

Your heart-strings cannot hold me.

I've decided I'm making new chapters my "hobby."
So If these beautiful memories we made together
happened to be our children-

Then thank you,

I'll be taking custody.

Ur my fantasy

The only way to fix my insecurity

Would be to have a mass extinction

Of every pretty girl,

Or every girl- except me

In existence

There are times that I feel beautiful

When I look in the mirror-

I fear, going out with others,

I might lose that glimmer.

I bet some of the stunners out there

Aren't just hotter than me but also cleverer.

I have my mirrors positioned now so

It looks as if I go on forever.

I like when I walk into a group of just men.

There's no need to compete

For the attention, to be more like the first and last woman they'll ever meet

With male eyes on me,

I feel more feminine.

I know that I want them to want me

Even if I don't want any of them.

I've reached a point

I'd probably best confess,

I don't want to be anything less

Amongst women than a pure bloody goddess.

While I'm at it - I've gotta say, I'd

like to walk through the halls

Of a prison one day.

Like a dream, I'd hypnotise

all the bad boy criminals.

They'd cry out to have little me,

The only woman within those walls.

Just gotta forget that

Though they're rattling their chains and making all
that noise-

They'd do that for any other girl

If they had the choice.

On the outside, at least how it feels-

Is that my fantasy will never be real

Because everywhere I look

When I leave my little world,

Is just another

more beautiful girl.

Ur unforgettable

Don't give me your mother fucking t-shirt to keep if you're
not going to give me your heart

Don't go giving me

Your boxers to wear

As if they're not yours

But ours

I'm not a charity shop

Donation box

act like you can't see me

so not to offend

Just don't buy me breakfast

in the morning

If you don't want to wake up

next to me again.

Ur my kryptonite

Fuck, I think I still miss you.

Fuck fuck fuck.

Wondering how many beers it

Would take for me to just

Give in and hit you up…

I still have your jumper,

I put it out of sight.

I am of course,

hung up right next to it-

I don't ever wear it out

But I wear it to bed some nights.

I wish I had a video of us fucking.

Then, maybe that would make it worse-

Fuck. I think I still want you. I want you- gift or curse.

You are without a doubt top 1 of all the men I've had,
that I'd kill

To have once more.

I also think you'd like the new me way more

than you said you could

You made me so sad before

But maybe I feel better now.

Maybe you were right, that I was wrong, and I was
only sad because of how desperately I needed
someone.

And maybe if we'd had longer, we'd have fully
bonded. I don't know how easy it will be to forgive
my sins. But I do know that
The devil comes dressed as
everything you've ever wanted.

Ur always on my mind

Little guardian angels

Have made their way into my life

In ways that people couldn't even dream

To find their future wives

I have a few special people in mind

Friends I could call them, though the thing
between us is all ours and all mine

The relationships you see in the movies exist

But with intricacies even the greatest

Director couldn't fix.

Its not how long you spend with them or

Your happily ever after.

It's the sequence of tableaux you have no choice
but to remember

Rich, vivid visions of tears and laughter.

I never really use the word

Acquaintance- though I definitely have loads.

But they are more to me than

Passers by- I keep noticing their shadows.

There are people I think of always

And some from time to time

There are some I think of never

But that still graced this little world of mine.

Forget about me if you want, because I won't
forget about you.

My life is a movie-

I choose the seat with a good view.

Loving is letting go,

Not everyone will feel the same

For me, distance makes the heart grow fonder-

And relationships never really end

They just change

Ur haunting

I would say

That I am Romantic

Not in practise but in theory

Actually I've practised loads-

I'm already always tired and it's starting to make
me weary…

I can feel like the main character,

With a world ahead of me and

No need to plan

But I'm not a good feminist

Sometimes instead I just want a man

Life's not about that,

I have to know I'll be fine.

That's what they tell me

Every

Single

Time

But is it too much to ask for

Longer than a week or a night?

Every time I get there I think that maybe I, you, we might.

Big lessons, sure- I win every time…

I look on the bright side but I still wish they were mine.

They've taught me to check my watch

And to keep checking my phone.

Now even when I'm with people

I feel like I'm the only one who's alone

I won't write texts

to people who don't give a fuck

until late at night when there's a chance I might
be up

I can't write poems about love

Though I want to the most

They are always about longing

Thanks to these all these ghosts

Ur such a tease

I love myself just fine okay

But fuck

Why can't you love me too

I've run my brain for ages over

What I did to scare you

I don't wanna hear it's because I put you on top

I went there too and you asked me

To please never stop

I can't see your face every time I close my eyes

I'm sick of feeling shitty every time another day goes by -

You keep your silence

As I wait for you to change your mind and

I try to convince myself you haven't been another body

Since you were in mine

I know by now that it's not about me

Just the place you're in

(Whatever loveless one that is)

You whispered to me that I was soft,

I smiled, you loved my grin

But somehow you still don't crave my skin

I shouldn't beg though if I could

I'd throw tantrum

When I want them back

They show me the back of them.

There's nothing to work on,

I don't need any mantras.

But now each time they walk away,

I just allow them.

Ur so cool

Puff puff puffing on my cigarettes.

You think it's gross and yucky.

Get yourself a cute little nicotine addiction

Then maybe you can talk,

Trust me.

You don't get it and you never will;

How I can ignore all the

STOP SMOKING IT WILL KILL YOUs

I do actually care-

It's not just a 'part of the thrill. '

Shame me and shame me, I know you will.

I choose not to give a fuck

Your judgment is what actually

made me feel disgusting

But it's that, I'm giving up.

I do want my health, I want the fresh air

But just like the wallowing artists

And the fucked up movie characters,

The cigarettes chose me

And made me theirs.

You're not actually better than me,

Get off your healthy little throne.

I'm not stupid, I'm just human

Nice heart you got there-

I've also still got my own.

I know what you'll say,

That I'm filling myself with shit

But in time of stress, don't you ever wish

It could evaporate in just a few

Minutes?

Yes, it's a filthy habit and terrible addiction.
Admitting it, I feel like a fool

But again, I'm a victim

of the denial that sometimes comes with the human
condition.

And to be fair, I'll admit this too:

I also maybe might think it's kind of cool.

Ur priceless to me

You put guitar picks on strings

with beads like the ones

from old friendship bracelets.

How did you turn them into

beautiful jewelry? Pearls of wisdom,

diamonds with the softest edges.

Rarer than some believed to be blood;

you dazzle without light

for reflection

and it hits me and I get the feeling

that there is an exception to rules

and you are the diamond

who's edges are smoothed without

needing another rock.

I'll wear you excitedly on Fridays.

Wildflower beds that bloom

effortlessly, how they were meant

have grown by the coloured lights you emit

and make me wonder if they were planted
specially for me

or if I made that up in my head.

Ur a dream

I don't know why but

Now I dream about the same guy

Nearly every single night-

When I google it

It's because he misses me

But I don't buy it

Actual years have passed

And marvellously you somehow

still seem

To be lurking in every

Single one of

my dreams

There I'm then main character

But you always get the role as antagonist

You were never that in

Real life to me-

until what I realised when

you vanished

Now it's the only way that you even exist.

I wouldn't say I miss you either.

But you're still such a big part of me

Because I learn from you

To this day

in my subconscious

Who's Ur Daddy?

Stop ruining my potential baby names

You fucks

I know too many boys with beautiful names

Who turned out to be shmucks

I can't call him Ethan

Though he doesn't exist

Because Ethan was a prick and that's

Just the start of my list:

Edward, obviously could have

Been a real prince Charming,

A future heartbreaker.

If he were my son that was-

but unfortunately, the first Ed

already got there

Gabe, Gabriel

Sounds so rare and soft

Though two of the three of them

left me at more than a loss.

Can't just shorten things

Because they already did it

If I used all their dumb nick names

I'd have to have triplets

Andy would be strong,

Treat women with care,

light up the room for everyone there

The Andy that ruined that

For any of my sons

Just used me as a play thing.

Don't think either of us found it fun

31

Charlie is cute, for a boy

Or a girl - a cool easy going one

They would make heads turn.

But 'Charlie' will only make

Me think of one specific

Male. Who won't have my son

Because we reached

An end to our little tale

Paul was creepy

And a bit too American

But that one wasn't even on my list

Because nobody

Should ever

Name their child

Paul

Ever Again

My child will be pure and their name bring good luck but

I'm running out of boys names

That haven't left me fucked.

While listing (some of) them out

And writing their names

For the first time in a while

I don't think they'd be to blame

If I raised my child

with their name

Into a better man

And to the standards I gained.

Though I'd rather they not know

That I think of their names

I have once more written them out.

Though they shat on every letter,

I forgive you all.

I just hope my son can do better.

Girl, R U From Pomeii?

Hidden under the ground

That others trampled until

she realised her greatest fear;

Now she erupts with an energy

That was dormant for years

Being a volcano that never erupted,

To be full but unfulfilled,

A mountain with potential it never discovered,
concealing its power

to kill

She moved like tectonic plates

When unexpected, she arrives-

She feared her legacy might never arise.

But then she gets even herself

With the element of surprise.

If she causes historic tragedies

Doesn't matter to her because

Every fairy tales has its flaws-

Every lion has its weakest paw.

And she'll go down in history,

No matter how tragic she was

That feeling when you've met a star

Was the one she had people get

When you wonder

"was that my future wife I just met?"

Unbeknown to her,

word spread of her charm,

She was the girl next door

Both near and far.

Cracked on the surface but underneath

 is where her journey was about to unleash.

An earthquake to shatter,

It's showing on their radars-

not long til she conquers, like Vesuvius.

She will erupt and just when

You might think its all going wrong-

You find out what she knew all along.

The screams of the city she crosses

will sound like the a chorus of a

Love song

Ur just like honey

Smooth and sweet,

Her voice on the phone

I can tell she's golden

Even more so since she's grown.

When she's thrown in the mix,

It's a kiss from a rose

And if she were honey she'd be the kind you get at
Waitrose

Just like Manuka,

She's noticeably rare

Sits glimmering on the shelf

For those, who know she's there

No image as beautiful since we sat, looking in the
oven, comparing our hair

We'd encourage each other but weren't fully aware

Of what it really meant

To have you around

As the perfect sweetener- gifted, not found

I could pay a pretty penny but

Be wasting my pounds

To try and ever buy a better bottle

Of the sweetest honey around

Ur so addictive

All these men are like cigarettes to me

I'll poison myself until I'm satisfied

They soothe me just briefly

I crave them day and night

especially at night

Because by myself, cold in my room

I just dream of the heat from their light

They fulfill their purpose

Then they go away

Their smoke surrounds me,

Suffocating me with euphoria

But when I try to catch it

It slips from my fingers anyway

We're symbiotic

But they tell me otherwise

And though it may not seem it;

They feed me sweet poison

So that maybe one day

I realise I don't need it

Ur so strong

I've realised that now I like olives, red wine

And the sound of Bjork's voice.

That I'd rather be at home with my thoughts and a fancy beer

Than with randoms amongst noise

I go to work with a skip in my step

I'm still late

But I pay my rent

And I work hard once I'm there

(And awake)

I have to calm my self down

Before I face my friends

And now I bloody journal

As like the only way to mend

I always want my hot water bottle,

If there isn't someone by my side.

I shower most evenings now…

Not just to avoid looking greasy but

For tomorrows sense of pride

I can walk myself down

London streets without light.

I don't always want to but

I tuck myself in at night.

I am an adult now I suppose

But ya know,
in my own right

People think I'm an old soul

Whatever that means.

Just the oldest one you've seen

In a crop top

And baggy jeans

Ur my goodluck charm

I thought foxes were nocturnal

Until I began seeing them always-

Thought maybe I was insane-

I don't know how it made sense

But you and them were the same

They became my good luck charm

When they followed me home

To the house I moved out of

before I met you.

Little did I know

The fox that found its way

To my door

Was giving me a lot more

than what I had been open to before

It had scurried

Across my path

Despite the obstacle course

How could it know to be

One of its kind?

When all sorts

Could approach

in the dark of night,

And with this city being so vast and wide.

Your goodness stands out- though you don't even try
and I feel lucky because these creatures are really
rare to find

We don't quite speak

The same language

But I love the way you talk.

These days they feel like

Guardian angels

When I catch them

As I walk

If you are them and they

Are you then

in my next life

Let me be a fox too

Ur so fit

I ran after you a couple times

And you mistook me for a chaser

You slowed down to see me,

You were moving at my pace first

You're quicker than me, by nature

and though, you got further away

I thought you might come back over

And see me another day

Instead I watched from the distance as you caught up to her

my heart was beating faster than usual and it was beginning to hurt

I wanted to be at the finish line and to see your face there

But I would hand in my number

Before placing second because I

I am no longer a racer

Ur kind is hard to come by

For romantics
like me,
the search for one
'exactly like me'
is a quest
on a road to nowhere
the long, lonely wander
is the most glorious journey
on which no other
soul has embarked

Ur just like breathing air

Sometimes I look around

I feel a bit present

Sound like a wanker

But I've learned to feel that way and let it

You realise that something you wished

In the back of your soul

Maybe recently

Or a very long time ago

Came true somehow

But little did you know

Just how amazing it would feel

When you live it in the present,

forget you're a massive wanker

And let go

9 789357 696500

Printed by BoD in Norderstedt, Germany